Original title:
Cocoa and Crackling Logs

Copyright © 2024 Creative Arts Management OÜ
All rights reserved.

Author: Arabella Whitmore
ISBN HARDBACK: 978-9916-94-406-6
ISBN PAPERBACK: 978-9916-94-407-3

## Moments Wrapped in Warmth

In a snug little nook, jokes take wing,
With mugs that giggle, and laughter to bring.
A sprinkling of sprinkles, a dollop of cheer,
Hot drinks in hand, the chill disappears.

Friends tell tall tales with marshmallows bold,
While stories of frosty fortresses unfold.
Each sip a chuckle, each laugh a delight,
In this cozy refuge, the world feels just right.

## The Magic of Stirring Stews

Behind the bubbling pot, mischief does play,
As wooden spoons dance, turning night into day.
A pinch of this, and a scoop of that,
Creates quite the ruckus, oh what of that spat?

Tomatoes in twirls, carrots in prance,
Dancing together in a rhythmic romance.
The broth hums a tune, a fragrant refrain,
As laughter erupts, like drops of warm rain.

## Fables of the Flickering Flame

The fire spins tales of great mustached beasts,
With shadows that twirl like delightful feasts.
They banter and giggle, in soft orange glow,
As the sparks join the party, with a flick and a show.

In the warmth of the hearth, we roast our delight,
While singed eyebrows get laughs—oh, what a sight!
With flames whispering secrets, mischief in tow,
We bask in the wonder, like kids in the snow.

## Aromatic Comforts and Warm Embrace

In the air wafts a hug, sweet and divine,
With spices and sugar, the world feels just fine.
Each sprinkle of cinnamon, a laugh sent our way,
In our merry cocoon, we simply sway.

Blankets piled high, like fortresses grand,
With giggles erupting, all perfectly planned.
Each moment a treasure, a giggle or sigh,
Wrapped in a smile, as the cold days float by.

## The Enchantment of Brewed Bliss

In a mug so round and warm,
Chocolate dreams take form.
Frothy mustaches, smiles wide,
Serenading winter's glide.

Slurps and giggles fill the air,
With friends who seem to care.
Every sip, a hearty scheme,
Laughter flows like a sweet dream.

## Sweetness in the Stillness

A sprinkle here, a swirl there,
Sassy sweetness in the chair.
Marshmallows bounce in delight,
As jokes fly like stars at night.

Each sip brings a tale to tell,
Of mishaps that we know too well.
Fumbling cups and a giggling spill,
In this moment, all is thrill.

## Fireside Memories and Rich Flavors

Crackling cheer and glowing glee,
Remind us how great friends can be.
One sip in, they start to jest,
With stories that bring out the best.

Firelight dances on our nips,
Unruly curls and chocolate drips.
Oh, how time morphs and bends,
With every laugh shared among friends.

## Glows and Aromas

Swooshing pots, a bubbling delight,
Steam rises into the starry night.
Charming scents swirl all around,
In this haven, joy is found.

Furry beasts by the hearthside lay,
Waiting for treats from this play.
Giggles spill with each donk and dunk,
As we toast to our fun-filled funk.

## **Nostalgic Sparks**

In a mug, a dance of steam,
With marshmallows floating like a dream.
Laughter bounces off the walls,
As memory's blanket softly calls.

Grandpa's tales, a little tall,
Of the time he tripped and made us all.
Pouring sweetness in the night,
Oh, how the stories take their flight.

Sipping warmth by the glow of the flame,
Silly jokes, we're all to blame.
Chocolate delights and friendly jabs,
Finding joy in our little drabs.

## Flicker and Flavor

The flicker of flames, a dance so bright,
Each pop an echo, a crackling delight.
With a spoon and a pot, we stir up cheer,
As friends come near with stories to share.

Whiskers twitch and chocolate spills,
Not a frown here, just laughter thrills.
Whimsical flavors swirl in a haze,
In this laughter-laden, chocolate phase.

Fingers sticky, we munch and giggle,
Sipping the brew, we laugh and wiggle.
Melting moments, we all agree,
Life's sweeter when shared with glee.

## The Warmth We Share

Under blankets thick, we sit in a row,
As the fire crackles with a vibrant glow.
Mismatched socks and silly hats,
All gather 'round for playful chats.

One's nose is red, a real sight to see,
Trying to guess who will spill their tea.
Giggles erupt, oh, what a mess!
But in this warmth, we feel so blessed.

Pajamas and smiles, oh what a crew,
Each sip of delight gives a happier hue.
We toast to the laughter, the fun we spark,
In our cozy corner, there's never a dark.

## Hearthside Harmony

With spoons in hand, we make a mess,
Swirling flavors, a culinary quest.
Jokes fly as cinnamon takes flight,
In our cheerful chaos, everything's right.

Chasing the giggles that bounce like a ball,
As crumbs of cookies are scattered on the wall.
Overflowing mugs, we share with glee,
Elixirs of joy, just you and me.

Catch that marshmallow before it flies,
Bouncing around like our little spies.
In the warmth where laughter breeds,
We find our magic, meeting all our needs.

## **Whispers of Warmth in the Air**

In the nook where laughter brews,
A mug of warmth, with silly views.
Sippin' joy by the crackling glow,
I swear my socks just danced, hello!

Marshmallows plop like fluffy clouds,
While giggles rise, dissolving shrouds.
A splash of cheer, a dash of smile,
And sticky fingers, oh, so worthwhile!

## **Rustic Fireside Reveries**

Logs piled high, a splintered crown,
The cat's in charge, she's wearing a gown.
Whiskers twitch, as shadows leap,
She swore she'd guard this cozy heap.

Crackles echo, woodsy tunes,
The hamster rolls out daydreams in runes.
I tell a tale, it's slightly bent,
And fuel the fire, with humor spent!

## Sweet Brews and Flickering Flames

A whirl of sweetness graces the mug,
A taste of mischief, a snug little hug.
Chocolates dance, a playful whirl,
As laughter springs, like a playful girl.

Spills and thrills, oh what a sight,
Even the spoon starts feeling bright.
With slurps and giggles, we share the fun,
Our hearts are warm, like the cozied sun!

## The Embrace of Spiced Delights

Stars twinkle bright in the chilly night,
While spices twirl, oh what a sight!
Laughter bubbles, a frothy tease,
As the night wraps round us, like a warm breeze.

Nuts crack open with merry glee,
A symphony bright as it rustles free.
We toast to joy, with every sip,
Each chuckle chirps on this wild trip!

## **Philosophies by Firelight**

When marshmallows dance in flames,
And wise socks tell their tales,
We ponder life's great questions,
While the cat starts to wail.

The chairs creak like old jokes,
As laughter fills the night,
A squirrel steals the popcorn,
Oh, what a silly sight!

With cocoa cups held high,
We toast to absent stars,
Each sip a secret flavor,
While sharing dreams of cars.

So drop the serious talk,
And let the silliness flow,
For wisdom found in giggles,
Is the best kind we know.

## Glimmers of Comfort

In the glow of flickering lights,
We reminisce on odd delights,
A raccoon in a top hat leaps,
As the laughter softly creeps.

Sippable spoons of frothy fluff,
Who knew it could be this tough?
With mugs that spill and spill again,
We giggle, let the mess descend.

The wind whispers funny tunes,
Like cats wearing silly spoons,
While snacks make a secret pact,
To avoid the dented act.

Wrap up in this cozy haze,
With chuckles that wander and graze,
Here in this warm, jester's den,
The fun begins, not just pretend.

## The Richness of Evening

The night wears a jester's cap,
Filled with jokes and childhood gags,
Each star twinkles a punchline,
As the moon plays with our rags.

With a fire that snaps and sparks,
We gather all our quirks and quirks,
Late-night snacks parade around,
In the twilight's playful sound.

So pass the silly stories 'round,
Like whispers shared and others found,
We'll crown the best of mishaps here,
With peanut butter and a beer.

In this merry little fest,
We find laughter's sweetest zest,
The richness of our evening lays,
In silly tunes and snacking ways.

## Sweet Melodies in the Air

A symphony of splashes sings,
From mugs that chip and clink,
As chocolate rivers flow beside,
We giggle 'bout what's in the drink.

The dog plays fetch with marshmallows,
While squirrels join in the show,
Each bounce is a note in harmony,
As the silly antics grow.

With crayons on the table now,
We craft a rainbow's cheer,
Drawing maps of our inventions,
And giggling without fear.

So let the sweet smells engulf us,
And the songs flow free and bright,
For in this laughter filled moment,
We spin the world outright.

## Brewed Conversations and Radiant Heat

In winter's chill, two mugs collide,
With jokes so rich, we laugh and hide.
A splash of cream, a sprinkle of spice,
Our giggles dance, oh, isn't this nice?

The kettle whistles, oh what a sound,
We share our tales, let the laughter abound.
Swirls of warmth fill the frosty air,
With puns so silly, we forget our care.

## Stories Flowing with Dark Richness

Once, a jester brewed up a plot,
A slip on the floor, oh, what a spot!
He spilled his brew on the table's face,
And made it a game, a charming disgrace.

Rich flavors rise with bubbles that swirl,
He twirled like a dancer, gave fate a whirl.
With each hearty laugh, the night grew bright,
As stories mingled, a most joyful sight.

**Charred Wood and Creamy Sips**

By the firelight, we sat with glee,
While marshmallows roasted, up-and-toasty.
A cat took a leap, the table shook,
And guess where it landed? Right in the nook!

We laughed at the chaos, the warm, sweet mess,
With nibbles and giggles, we felt so blessed.
As embers glowed brighter, we went for more,
Each sip added warmth, as joys we'd implore.

## **Lunar Reflections in a Mug**

Under the moonlight, two friends convene,
With tales full of laughter, a delightful scene.
The mugs held secrets, both frothy and bold,
While stories of clumsiness were proudly retold.

The silver orb shone, laughter erupted,
As marshmallows danced, and silly strings erupted.
In the night's embrace, we savored each drop,
With joy overflowing, we'd never stop.

## The Dance of Frost and Flame

In the chill of winter's lock,
A pot begins to rock.
With a splatter and a pop,
It makes us laugh non-stop.

Marshmallows on a stick,
Roasting oh so quick.
With each gooey delight,
We giggle with pure delight.

The snowflakes swirl and bend,
As we dance, no end.
Spinning 'round like fools,
Breaking all the rules.

And when the flames grow low,
Just watch our faces glow.
In this cozy, warm retreat,
Life's little joys can't be beat.

## Ember's Whisper

A spark jumps high, plays a prank,
While we fill our cups from the tank.
Laughter floats like the steam,
In this warming, cheesy dream.

The logs crackle, pop, and hiss,
Like secrets wrapped in fizzy bliss.
Each sip warms the silly soul,
As we joke and lose control.

With quirky hats and silly cheers,
We sip away our burning fears.
The night's a canvas, bright with fun,
Under so many twinkling suns.

When the chill creeps near, we know
To laugh, to dance, let good times flow.
In whispers soft, our hearts will sing,
The joy that playful moments bring.

## Cake and Warm Spirits

Fluffy layers stacked up high,
Like a tower reaching sky.
With frosting slick and nuts to nibble,
We laugh and cheer and start to giggle.

As candles flicker, we take a bite,
Each crumb a cause for delight.
With every mouthful we can't muffle,
The chatter and the playful scuffle.

A sip here, a bite there,
Who knew sweets could lead to flair?
A sugar rush, a burst of cheer,
In this festive, cozy sphere.

Then crumbs adorn like shiny stars,
As we share joy beneath the jars.
So here's to laughter, love, and cake,
In every moment, memories we make.

## A Simple Refuge Under the Stars

Wrapped in blankets, here we lie,
The twinkling jewels in the sky.
Tell me tales of far-off lands,
With silly dreams and laughter on strands.

The crickets chirp a funny song,
While shadows dance and sway along.
Oh, the warmth of friendships near,
Makes any night a time to cheer.

In this refuge, we share our quirks,
Chat away with playful smirks.
Each star a giggle, pure and bright,
Beneath the blanket of night.

So raise a cup, let's toast to fun,
The stories told, adventures spun.
With laughter echoing far and wide,
In this cozy spot, we take our pride.

## **Velvet Warmth**

In a mug of joy, steam does rise,
A swirl of mischief hides in disguise.
Giggles bounce off the chilly air,
Sipping bliss, without a care.

Laughter crashes like the gentle waves,
Sweet delights that everyone craves.
With marshmallows soft, they dance and float,
In a sea of laughter, we all gloat.

Chubby cheeks, all rosy bright,
With every sip, we take to flight.
A toast to friends, and tasty cheer,
In this warmth, we shed our fear.

So raise your cups, let spirits soar,
In this cozy land, there's always more.
With every drop, hilarity clings,
As we sip and share, our joy sings.

## The Dancing Flames

Flickering tongues reach out to tease,
Crackling whispers on the winter breeze.
They spin and jump, a lively show,
As shadows perform in a playful glow.

With every snap, a comic spark,
They flirt and flirt, igniting the dark.
Holding court, with sparks of cheer,
Prancing around, they draw us near.

Laughter rises, the room takes flight,
The flames are jesters, a pure delight.
Their crackling giggles, a merry tune,
In this little dance, all hearts attune.

So lean in close, and catch the fun,
Let the joy of warmth weigh a ton.
With playful flames, our chuckles burn,
In this bright whirl, we take our turn.

## Chocolate Dreams by the Hearth

In the cozy corner, dreams take shape,
With frothy frolics and sweet escape.
Honeyed whispers in the air,
Adventures shake off winter's stare.

With each cupped warmth, delights arise,
Chasing giggles, beneath dark skies.
Imagined lands where flavors blend,
The laughter twirls, our hearts extend.

Sudden bursts like tiny glee,
Rich with wonder, wild and free.
Mischief dances on every sip,
With chocolate rivers, let's take a trip!

So grab a seat, don't let it cool,
Join the fest, let spirits rule.
With every sip, let laughter beam,
In this warm glow, we dare to dream.

## Ember Glows and Sweet Brews

In the glow of night, magic brews,
A pinch of fun and silly hues.
Embers chuckle, a gentle tease,
Whispering tales that aim to please.

Tiny bubbles jump and swirl,
In the pot where flavors twirl.
Jokes collide like playful peas,
Each little sip, a bit of ease.

With giggly friends gathered near,
Tickled by warmth, we shed our fear.
Flowing jokes like a winding stream,
In this fun mix, we laugh and dream.

So toast to warmth and joyful chats,
As we sip away our silly spats.
With ember glows, let laughter fuse,
In this cozy haven, we can't lose!

## Hearth Hymns and Warmth's Glow

In the room where warmth unfolds,
Laughter dances, stories told.
A mug in hand, smiles ignite,
Even shadows seem to delight.

Footsteps shuffle, dogs prance near,
Puppy eyes glint with not a fear.
The wind outside sings a chilly tune,
While we cozy up, a rounded spoon.

Friends gather round, a playful tease,
Hot splashes land, oh what a breeze!
Mirth fills the air like marshmallow fluff,
Who knew warmth could also be tough?

With each crackle, giggles rise,
Like fireflies dancing in the skies.
Here we are, so snug and free,
A night like this? A pure jubilee!

## A Cup of Joy by Flames

A splash of cream on frothy peaks,
As laughter bubbles, friendship speaks.
Silly hats and mismatched socks,
Joy pours out like melting rocks.

Slippers squeak and socks collide,
Dance moves poor, yet we smile wide.
With warmth that wraps like a soft embrace,
Even the dogs join in this race.

Cookies comically, a bit too brown,
We munch with glee, not a single frown.
Each bite a giggle, a shared delight,
Within our hearts, the fire ignites.

Chilly winds try to sneak inside,
But with our crew, there's nothing to hide.
We sip our drinks as the night does call,
With cheer and laughter, we conquer all!

## **Steamy Conversations Under Stars**

Beneath the night, stars dancing bright,
Chit-chat bubbles, all feels so right.
A little secret, a wink and nod,
As marshmallows tumble from the odd.

Sipping something warm, oh what a sip,
Our stories twist like a joyful trip.
Jokes fly high as the fire crackles,
Why do the squirrels have such funny tackles?

Hey! Did you see that clever raccoon?
His antics could make the whole world swoon.
We giggle under the twinkling sky,
As the flames flicker and sparks fly high.

A time to cherish, a moment to hold,
With friends around, we're never cold.
The night hums sweetly, we're lost in the glow,
In this beautiful mess, we continue to flow!

## Soft Light and Sweet Fragrance

In a glow that glimmers, soft and neat,
Laughter and nostalgia find their seat.
The smell of sugar fills the air,
As we share tales with extravagant flair.

Sloppy sips and scattered crumbs,
Every burst of laughter hums.
Cats on laps, dogs in a heap,
In this chaos, our spirits leap.

Near the flames, we spin our dreams,
Like silly puppets in joyful schemes.
Chasing shadows, we twist and twine,
With each crackle, our hearts align.

An accidental splash and a fragrant cloud,
As we sing silly songs, so joyful and loud.
In this warmth, we truly belong,
Wrapped in each other, forever strong.

## Hearthside Tales

By the fire we share our jest,
A tale that puts our giggles to the test.
Fluffy marshmallows fly up high,
As squirrels dodge our laughter in the sky.

The toast pops up, a prancing dance,
Even two left feet can take a chance.
Slipping slips and buttery spills,
Chasing laughter up the hills.

We toast to friends, to fun and cheer,
While shadows twist and disappear.
With every chuckle, the warmth ignites,
In this whimsical world of cozy delights.

## Celestial Chocola

Stars alight on crispy treats,
As we munch on the best of sweets.
Chocolate shimmies, it starts to melt,
In our hands, pure joy is felt.

The moon peeks in with a sly little grin,
As nuts and sprinkles take a spin.
A puppet show of spoons and bowls,
Creating laughter that tickles souls.

We craft our laughs with every bite,
In this tasty dream, all feels right.
When we raise our cups to the midnight sky,
Sweet chaos reigns, oh my, oh my!

## Toasted Mirth

With crispy chatter around the flame,
We roast our tales, none are the same.
Giggles hop from ember to edge,
As we cross this weird, tasty pledge.

S'mores are squishy, laughter flows,
With chocolate dribbles and sticky toes.
Oh what a scene, our merry crew,
Dancing crumbs, sad but true!

The night is ours, the delight expands,
As each shared humor, like grains of sand.
We build our giggles, layer by layer,
Proving friendship's the sweetest affair!

## Twinkle Lights and Fudge Nights

Beneath the glow of cheerful rays,
We bundle up in laughter's daze.
Candies twinkle, gleaming bright,
As we munch and chuckle through the night.

Sprinkles tumble like starlit rain,
Leaving trails of giggles in our brain.
Sausage curls and jelly bean fights,
In this wacky world of silly delights.

We throw our treats high in the air,
As dreams mix with giddy flair.
With a wink and a nod, we take a bite,
In this festive dream, everything's just right!

## **Brewed Tales and Soft Glows**

In a cup so warm, a tale unfolds,
With marshmallows bobbing, and laughter bold.
A spoon takes a dive, a splash and a grin,
Oh, the chaos that brews beneath the frothy skin.

Bubbles are giggling, like secrets they spill,
Whispers of sweetness, a delicious thrill.
Each sip is a joy, a smile in disguise,
Crafted for fun, under wintery skies.

Stirred visions of snowmen, with noses so bright,
Dance in the warmth, on this cozy night.
A frosty challenge, the mug will not yield,
While friends share their stories, with joy unconcealed.

So raise up your drinks and toast to the cheer,
For moments like these are the ones we hold dear.
With laughter and warmth, we'll fill every space,
In brewed tales and soft glows, we find our embrace.

## Drafts of Dreams and Warm Light

In a kettle's embrace, the steam starts to rise,
With fingers a-dance, and a glint in our eyes.
A pinch of mischief, a dash of delight,
Sippin' our dreams, on this whimsical night.

Frothy concoctions, with flavors galore,
A swirl of the pumpkin, and spice to explore.
The mugs are our canvas, as giggles unfold,
In drafts of our dreams, no tales left untold.

Laughter erupts like the warmth of a glow,
With winks at each other, and jokes thrown below.
A gingerbread army, a legion in sight,
All staged for the fun, in this magical light.

So let every sip bring a chuckle and cheer,
In warmth of the moments, our hearts are sincere.
With drafts of our dreams, let the mischief ignite,
And treasure the giggles that fill up the night.

## Spirits Rising with the Flames

As fire crackles softly, we gather around,
With stories all ready, our laughter is loud.
The snacks are all scattered, a feast for the bold,
With drinks overflowing, the warmth to behold.

Roasted marshmallows, they wobble and sway,
In this merry madness, they dance and they play.
Each bite a delight, laughter spills from our lips,
As spirits are lifted in warm, hearty sips.

Jokes bounce like popcorn, as flames flicker high,
While shadows are dancing like stars in the sky.
The fun multiplies with each toast we share,
In moments so bright, filled with joy and care.

So let's sip and giggle, and savor the cheer,
With spirits all rising, our hearts ever near.
In warmth of the flames, let our laughter proclaim,
That life's sweetest moments are never the same.

## The Cozy Essence of Winter

In blankets we're bundled, with mugs in our hands,
Reflecting on winter with chatter so grand.
The night comes alive with the crackle and pop,
As joy floods the room, and we never want to stop.

A dance with the shadows, a twirl of delight,
With each cheeky story, the cold feels just right.
The essence of cozy fills in every nook,
As warmth weaves its magic, like the best kind of book.

We stoke up the fire, with laughter as fuel,
Like elves in the night, we play by our rule.
The season's a canvas, painted bright with cheer,
In our corners of bliss, winter's charms reappear.

So share in this warmth, let's embrace every laugh,
With cups overflowing, let's weave our own path.
In the cozy essence, we find ways to play,
And cherish the moments that brighten our day.

## Flickering Shadows of Home

In the corner, the cat does prance,
With leaps and bounds, a wild dance.
The fire pops, a comic show,
As shadows stretch and sway below.

A mug that's warm, a grin so wide,
You'd think it's tea, but that's a lie.
It's just a potion, mix it right,
For giggles in the dead of night.

The dog snores loud, a tiny beast,
While visions of treats dance in his feast.
The logs do crackle, they speak of cheer,
As laughter echoes, year after year.

So raise a toast, to times delight,
With snacks and fun, oh what a sight!
For home is where the whimsies bloom,
In cozy corners, laughter's room.

## **Beneath a Blanket of Stars**

On a cushy chair, I sink so deep,
With snacks so sweet, I hardly sleep.
The night sky twinkles, full of glee,
While critters scurry, oh so free.

Jokes fly around like fluffy sheep,
As everyone laughs, and ruckus we keep.
The warmth surrounds us, a friendly glow,
With stories shared where giggles flow.

A silly dance, an accidental trip,
As I reach for that chocolaty dip.
The marshmallows float, a buoyant crew,
Caught in the sweetness of the view.

In the distance, an owl hoots loud,
While we create our joyous crowd.
Under the stars, we find our tune,
In this cozy night, we're over the moon.

## Sips of Serenity

A mug in hand, I sip so slow,
As laughter bubbles, high and low.
The steam curls up, a fragrant hug,
While jokes fly around like a playful bug.

The kettle whistles, music to my ears,
With splashes of humor that bring out cheers.
Tiny marshmallows bobbing near,
Each one a giggle, each sip a cheer.

A funny face, a playful jest,
In the warmth of friends, we feel so blessed.
The night unfolds with tales that seize,
The simple moments that bring us ease.

So fill your cup, and join the fun,
For with each laugh, our hearts do run.
In the glow of warmth and blissful sip,
We find pure joy in every trip.

**Rustic Retreats**

In a rustic nook, where laughter roams,
With goodies piled in playful homes.
The fire crackles, it tells a tale,
Of silly antics, we never fail.

That chair is lopsided, but who would care?
As stories unfold, we're unaware.
Of time that slips, we're lost in mirth,
In this comfy spot, we find our worth.

Tea spills slightly, with giggles it flows,
As friends turn to jesters, everyone knows.
The warmth embraces, like a cozy shawl,
While antics abound, we're having a ball.

So here's to the nights, and memories made,
Where laughter and warmth will never fade.
In rustic retreats, our hearts collide,
With joy in abundance, and friends beside.

## Inviting Heat and Rich Textures

In the chill of the evening air,
We gather 'round, without a care.
Chubby cheeks and cozy attire,
With smiles that dance, our hearts on fire.

Sips of warmth in our little mugs,
Each slurp brings giggles, warm hugs.
The chairs do creak, a cheerful sound,
As timeless tales of fun abound.

Sticky fingers, we snatch a treat,
With laughter, nibbles can't be beat.
The way they melt, it's pure delight,
As we share jokes that last all night!

Around the flame, shadows leap,
As our giggles start to creep.
With every crack, we share our tales,
In this playful warmth, love prevails.

## Fireside Lullabies and Foamy Dreams

Under a blanket, snug and tight,
We roast with glee, a comical sight.
The logs they pop, a mischievous snap,
As we snuggle in our cozy lap.

Fireside chatter, jokes take flight,
While marshmallow monsters dance in the light.
With eyes that twinkle, we share a grin,
As chocolate rivers pour, let the fun begin!

The warmth envelops, perfect embrace,
With laughter echoing, a silly race.
To catch the sweetness, we play and slip,
Caught in a treat's delightful grip.

Frothy wonders in our hands,
As giggles float like sparkling bands.
With stories spun and hearts aglow,
We revel in joy, let the good times flow.

## Swirls of Spice and Laughter

In this room, the scent runs wild,
Like a giant playground for a child.
The spices swirl, a jesters' dance,
In steaming cups, we find our chance.

Each twirl, a giggle, each sip, a cheer,
We cuddle closer, without fear.
The warmth surrounds us, silly grins,
As each cheeky joke always wins.

Pine logs crackle, like laughter's song,
With playful banter, we all belong.
Marshmallows toast in a silly race,
With each gooey bite, we share our space.

As the night deepens, the lights grow dim,
Our chatter fades to a whimsical whim.
In this bubble of fun, we know it's true,
Warm memories wrapped, just me and you.

## The Alchemy of Warmth

Gathered 'round, the laughter flows,
As mischief stirs, everyone knows.
Each mug a potion, bubbling bright,
In this humorous blend, pure delight.

The dance of flavor, notes collide,
With every sip, our spirits ride.
Furry socks and silly hats,
Warmth and joy, we share like cats.

Chaotic moments, marshmallow might,
With sticky fingers, it all feels right.
In snippets of toast, silly shouts,
Each bubbly laugh a colorful bout.

So raise a toast to cozy bliss,
In this warm haven, we reminisce.
With logs a-crackle and spirits high,
We find our play beneath the sky.

## Savoring the Heat of Winter

In the chill of frosty air,
I stomp and clap with a flair.
A mug of warmth, a joyful cheer,
Who needs a beach? I've got this here.

The snowflakes fall, a dance of white,
But inside, I'm snug and feeling bright.
My drink's a potion, laughter it brings,
As I toast to snowmen and funny things.

Each sip's a tale, a giggle, a grin,
Like toddler snowballs tossed in a spin.
With every gulp, I chuckle and cheer,
Winter's folly is merrily here.

So let it snow, let the cold winds blow,
In my cozy nook, I'm stealing the show.
Raise your mug and let's make a toast,
To melted marshmallows and warmth we boast!

## Aromas of the Night's Refuge

Evening creeps with a playful sigh,
Shadows dance beneath the sky.
The aroma swirls with a wink and grin,
It's a spicy treat—let the fun begin.

With each waft, the stories unfold,
Of marshmallow battles, daring and bold.
The fire flickers, a mischievous spark,
As we laugh 'til the skies go dark.

Oh, the giggles rise like steam from cups,
In our fortress of warmth, we're cozy chumps.
The night is young, and spirits flare,
With twinkling lights and laughter in air.

Each sip a treasure, let's share the delight,
With flavors that twinkle, hearts feeling light.
So grab a friend, let's bask in this glow,
For in this refuge, our joy will flow!

## With Each Sip, the Fire Dances

A crackle, a pop, and a hearty laugh,
Fueling the flames, our bubbling gaff.
I take a sip, then nearly spill,
As the marshmallow takes the thrill!

The warmth wraps 'round like a fuzzy hug,
While stories leap like a playful bug.
Fumbling fingers, a chocolate dash,
Oh dear, there goes the tasty splash!

Beneath the flickers, we find our mirth,
Each sip a giggle, a burst of worth.
So pass around the drink so sweet,
And let's toast to laughter, a winter treat!

With every drop, our spirits rise,
Around the hearth, our joy complies.
In this merry scene, we dance and sing,
To the magic that winter nights can bring!

## Dark Elixirs and Glowing Embers

In shadows deep, where warmth does flow,
A potion brews that steals the show.
Dark elixirs with laughter to share,
Sparkling joy, like a comet's flare.

With spoons in hand, we mix and stir,
Lively tales, and much prefer.
The flames leap high, the embers glow,
As we play games of 'who wants more?'

A sip of cheer, a dash of glee,
At this fireplace, we all agree.
Snores and chuckles fill the air,
As sweet aromas weave and dare.

So let's be merry by the light,
Our hearts warm up, feeling just right.
In a swirl of flavors, we find our cheer,
It's more than a drink—it's friendship here!

## Chocolaty Whispers

In a cup so rich and round,
A secret flavor can be found.
It's sweeter than a dancing bear,
With frothy clouds to brush your hair.

A squirrel sips in little sips,
While wearing tiny, chocolate lips.
He tells of nutty tales so bright,
As marshmallows take to lofty flight.

A giggle bursts from steaming mugs,
That full of mischief, bounces hugs.
With every swirl, a laugh sets free,
The joy of warmth, oh let it be!

When brown and creamy streams unite,
The world seems silly, pure delight.
So come and join this frothy dream,
In the world of laugh and sweetened cream.

## Fireside Fables

In glowing corners, tales unfold,
Of talking nuts that can be bold.
With crackling voices, soft and sly,
They share their tales while heroes fly.

A fire crackles, all ablaze,
As hedgehogs dance in fiery rays.
Their tiny feet in shadows play,
While puppies sing the night away.

The charred marshmallows cheer and shout,
While popcorn's laughter roams about.
With every pop, a story grows,
Of chocolate rivers, slippered toes.

So gather 'round, put worries down,
For fables spun will wear a crown.
With giggles shared beside the heat,
Each tale's a treat, let's take a seat!

## Warm Brews and Ember Glow

With every sip, a spark ignites,
A giggle dances, sweet delights.
In cozy chairs where stories flow,
We sip the warmth, we feel the glow.

A bear who wears a polka dot,
Mixes berries in the pot.
His mustache twirls with every taste,
As friends devour with merry haste.

The rabbits gather, tails so grand,
To swirl and froth with keen demand.
A sprinkle here, a splash of that,
With laughter, they all tip their hat.

So let the embers crack a tune,
As steamy cups hold hearts in swoon.
For every brew, a punchline waits,
As joy spills over, lovely mates.

## Sips of Comfort by the Hearth

A cozy nook where flavors soar,
With every sip, we laugh some more.
The throw pillows whisper jovial songs,
And chatter about where everyone belongs.

A cat in slippers purrs and sways,
While dreaming of fish and sunny rays.
His whiskers twitch at the furry fun,
As chocolate streams light up the sun.

Laughter bubbles up like cream,
As everyone joins the playful scheme.
The cups clink loud in harmony,
To warm hearts close, a symphony.

So cozy up, stay for a while,
Let every sip invite a smile.
With whispered tales and frothy cheer,
Find joy in sips, oh bring it near!

## Flickering Shadows and Comforting Brews

In the corner, a chair, quite worn,
Squeaks and groans, a voice reborn.
A mug full of laughter, warmth inside,
As shadows dance, our worries slide.

With every sip, the chuckles grow,
The room is aglow with a frothy show.
Snickers and giggles, oh what a blend,
This cozy circus, where jokes never end.

Pancakes flip-flop like rubbery fish,
Syrup spills over, oh what a wish!
The mishaps tumble, but we're all in glee,
In our little world, mischief runs free.

So gather 'round friends, let laughter take flight,
In cozy corners, all feels just right.
With blessed banter and hearty cheer,
We'll toast to the moments we hold so dear.

## The Art of Warmth and Spice

A pot on the stove, bubbles like dreams,
Mixing up flavors, or so it seems.
A dash of giggles, a pinch of cheer,
It's a tasting party, come join us here!

With every twist, the spices fight,
Who can create the best tonight?
A spoonful of mischief, a sprinkle of fun,
In our culinary battle, we all can't just run.

The toast pops up, like a little surprise,
Burned edges laugh, much to our eyes.
We'll spread on the stories, and butter too,
As we reminisce over mishaps we grew.

Gather with friends, stir memories bright,
In flavors and friendships, we find pure delight.
The art of reunion, it warms the soul,
With debacles of dinner, we all play a role.

## Hearthside Bliss and Stories Unfolded

On a knit blanket, we sit and spin tales,
Of long-ago travels and windy gales.
The fire pops, the sparks take flight,
As laughter echoes into the night.

The chocolate fountains flow with bright glows,
While everyone wonders just where it goes.
Mischievous sips make faces distort,
In this gathering space, we find our report.

With marshmallows dancing over the heat,
We roast silly jokes as we share a sweet treat.
Chin up and smiles, when stories collide,
A tapestry woven with love, side by side.

So let the embers whisper their secrets near,
In the warmth of connection, we conquer the fear.
Hearthside together, like butter and jam,
We savor the stories, with love, yes we can!

## **Blazing Hearths and Rich Delights**

The fire roars, like a wild beast,
While laughter tumbles, a joyful feast.
Chocolate rivers and giggles arise,
In our sacred space, see the joy in our eyes.

Crackling embers, bright and bold,
A comedy show, our warmth unfolds.
Dough on our shirts and flour in hair,
We don't mind the mess; it's all in the air.

As stories tumble like snacks on a plate,
We brew up delight, there's never too late.
With each splash of whimsy and bursts of cheer,
We're rolling in laughter, it's our favorite sphere.

So laugh with us, friends, come huddle so close,
In the blaze of joy, we raise our toast.
With sips of wonder and warmth to bestow,
We twirl in our moments, letting laughter flow.

## Fireside Mirth and Sweet Brews

With marshmallows afloat, we giggle and grin,
The jokes are as soft as the warmth from within.
A cup full of cheer, bubbles tickle the nose,
As we trade silly tales in our fuzzy warm clothes.

That chair creaks like laughter, it joins in the fun,
Our socks are mismatched, oh, how we have spun!
From fairy tales told to the mishaps we share,
The fire dances brightly, we haven't a care.

A splash of hot joy, as moonlight breaks through,
The shadows are painted in shades of bright hue.
We orphan our worries, let spirits run free,
In bubbling delight, we are silly as can be.

So here's to the evening of antics galore,
With giggles and warmth, who could ask for more?
With each hearty sip, our hearts hover near,
In the glow of the night, we celebrate cheer!

## Tales Traced in Warmth

Gather 'round, dear friends, as the night's stories flow,
Of clumsy old cats and the cheese thief we know.
A cozy retreat in this warm, glowing space,
Where laughter erupts like a spiced-drink embrace.

With each regal sip, we recount our grand quests,
How socks disappear, joining mismatched vests.
The twinkle of embers winks back with delight,
As we share silly scrapes 'til the dawn's early light.

In the warmth of our circle, the giggles ignite,
As shadows grow longer, our minds take to flight.
A mug filled with wonder, spiced with our jest,
Generates warmth that we treasure the best.

These tales wrapped in laughter become sweet brigade,
With heartwarming sips, it's a magical trade.
So here in the glow, let all worries retreat,
For joy found in company is truly a treat!

## The Spell of a Scented Mug

A mug here, a mug there, each filled to the brim,
With flavors that tingle, and our voices whim.
The gentle wind whispers through branches and leaves,
As we chuckle at tales of our holiday grieves.

With every warm sip, an odd dance takes shape,
While stories take flight of a cat and a cape.
The giggles erupt like bubbling sweet brews,
As steam wraps us warmly, sprinkling sweet news.

So let's toast to the moments, the fun and the mist,
Of smearing up faces with marshmallows kissed.
In the light of the flames, our laughter takes wing,
Each sip is a spark, in delight we shall sing!

In this cozy retreat, where our spirits can play,
The warmth feeds our souls, drives the chill far away.
With cups raised high, here's our nonsensical cheer,
In a timeless embrace, we hold the night near!

## **Rustic Charms and Leafy Whirls**


In the twinkling glow, the giggles take flight,
With stories of squirrels and how they dance right.
The night's magic brews in a wobbly mug,
As chaos ensues, like a played-out snug bug.

Who knew that a cup could spark such delight?
With splashes of joy that go bump in the night.
A ticklish warm feeling ignites in the dark,
Where laughter and tales leave a special sweet mark.

Through rustic charms, we relish each cheer,
Holding close delightful sips, banishing fear.
The foliage sways with a whimsical dance,
As we sip our concoctions, lost in sweet trance.

Let's toast to the whimsy that life has to give,
Where laughter's our fuel, and together we live.
With nudges and winks in our warm little nook,
We weave the night magic like a storybook!

## Essence of Winter Warmth

Beneath a blanket, snug and tight,
A mug of cheer, my heart's delight.
The snowflakes dance like they're so bold,
While I sip warmth, in tales retold.

A dash of spice, a frothy cream,
In laughter shared, we softly beam.
With marshmallows soft, a little treat,
We cozy up, oh what a feat!

The chill outside can take a seat,
For inside here, it's quite the heat.
As laughter cracks like fire's glow,
Our hearts entwined, with joy we flow.

So let the winter do its worst,
We're armed with warmth, we're truly cursed.
To know such joy, on this fine night,
With silly tales and sheer delight.

## Woodland Brews

In woods so deep where shadows play,
We brew our fun, oh what a sway!
The critters watch with curious eyes,
As we concoct our tasty pies.

A pinch of giggles, a sprinkle of cheer,
A hint of mischief, oh so near.
With every sip, our laughter grows,
And woodland friends join in the prose.

The kettle sings, a merry tune,
While swirls of steam dance like the moon.
The birds join in, a chirpy choir,
To celebrate the warmth we desire.

So raise your mugs to tree and sky,
For woodland fun will never die.
In every sip, we share our glee,
A brew of laughter, wild and free.

## Heartfelt Roast

Gather 'round the hearth tonight,
With friends we share our warm delight.
The fire crackles, soft and bright,
While stories spill with sheer delight.

A roast of humor, spices bold,
In every laugh, a tale retold.
With faces flushed and voices raised,
Our silly antics leave us dazed.

The flames flicker, as shadows play,
We bring the night, and set the sway.
A cozy hug, a friendship toast,
The heart's warm glow, we cherish most.

So here's to nights of joy and cheer,
To heartfelt moments we hold dear.
With laughter and love, we become whole,
In every jest, we warm the soul.

## Eternal Solace

When winter winds begin to howl,
We gather close, we laugh and scowl.
With stilly mugs and brightened smiles,
Our souls entwined through endless miles.

Each sip and giggle, light as air,
A fest of warmth, beyond compare.
With chocolate dreams, we twirl and dance,
In moments filled with silly chance.

Outside the frost may fiercely bite,
But here inside, it's pure delight.
With playful banter, whimsies bloom,
As we embrace the cozy room.

So let the frost take all its gain,
For we will thrive through joy and pain.
In every laugh, we find our peace,
With every toast, our sweet release.

## Flicker and Foam

In the corner a kettle sings so bright,
Whistling tunes in the pale moonlight.
Pots dance on the stove, what a sight,
While I just try not to spill my fright.

Marshmallows giggle, float without care,
Each one a cloud in this warm air.
With a spoon as my scepter, I declare,
That laughter fills the room, oh, where?

Stirring the pot, a swirl of delight,
The bubbles bounce high, a silly flight.
Spatters and splashes, what a plight,
My apron a canvas, oh what a sight!

With each sip, the world starts to sway,
As the flames compete with what I say.
Who knew that warmth could be this way?
Let mischief reign till the break of day!

## Toasted Moments Beneath the Stars

Under a blanket of sparkling night,
We roast stories as the fire burns bright.
Popcorn jumps, and tries to take flight,
Each kernel a prankster, oh what a fright!

Sipping sweet nectar from vessels of cheer,
We toast to the chaos, our laughter clear.
With each crackle, new jokes appear,
While the shadows seem to dance near.

Furry companions beg near our feet,
Eyes wide as if they're part of the feat.
But they just want those crumbs that we treat,
While we munch and crunch, oh, what a sweet!

So here we giggle and munch with delight,
Under twinkling stars, everything feels right.
With each story shared and snickered slight,
These toasted moments shine through the night!

## Melodies of Mocha and Wood

Crackling warmth hums a cozy song,
A symphony where we all belong.
Stirrings and chirps, the night dances long,
While we plot the silliest, teasing throng.

Beans grind away for a potion so fine,
A swirling blend as we toast with wine.
Each sip inspires a joke or a line,
While banter bubbles like sweetened brine.

With mugs held high, we cheer and jest,
In this festival of fun, we are blessed.
Flames leap and dive, a flaming quest,
All wrapped in moments we love the best!

So join the revelry, don't be shy,
With every chuckle, watch worries fly.
In this melody where we all vie,
The night paints laughter in the sky!

## Hearthside Dreams and Drink

Gather 'round the hearth, the tales unfold,
As marshmallows melt into laughter bold.
Every pop from the fire is gold,
While secrets mingle and stories are told.

A sip of the brew, sweet and divine,
Happiness bubbles in every line.
With friends all around, we intertwine,
As the glow of the flames starts to shine.

Eyes twinkle bright like the stars above,
In this cozy nook, we find our love.
Every slurp and giggle, a little shove,
Brings us closer; oh, what a glove!

So let's dream and sip, let the good times ring,
Underneath this roof, let's dance and sing.
For hearthside moments are our favorite thing,
In a world of joy, let's take wing!

## Serenading the Night with Sips

Under the stars we shimmied and twirled,
With mugs in hand, our laughter unfurled.
The warmth wrapped us tight, like a silly old coil,
As we spilled our dreams in a chocolatey spoil.

Sips turned to giggles, rich sweetness did flow,
Who knew a warm drink could steal the show?
Slips on the rug made the evening a blast,
With sprinkles of chaos, our fun was amassed.

Oh, the crunchy delight that we shared on that night,
Every sip a story, every laugh pure delight.
As shadows danced wildly and flickered their beams,
We toasted to joy, wrapped in our dreams.

So here's to the mugs and the laughter they bring,
To nights full of fun that make the heart sing.
With silliness swirling and spirits that soar,
We'll sip and we'll giggle forever, and more.

## A Hearth of Wishes and Warm Tastes

In the glow of the fire, we gathered around,
With wishes and whispers, our laughter unbound.
A brewing concoction so vibrant and sweet,
We toasted our toes by the warm, cozy heat.

With a sprinkle of mischief, we clinked our fine cups,
And danced with the marshmallows, oh, what sort of pups!
A giggle erupted, we spilled all the cream,
As memories bubbled like a sweet silly dream.

The shadows were playmates, with faces aglow,
As we sipped on our wishes, letting delight flow.
A hearth full of wonder, with flavors that tease,
While chuckles and grins put our worries at ease.

So let's raise our mugs to the warmth that we find,
With funny little tales, and joy intertwined.
For every warm sip, let the good times ignite,
A cheer for the silly, on this whimsical night.

## Cozy Shadows and Inviting Brews

In the heart of the evening, shadows leapt high,
With giggles and warmth, like puffs in the sky.
Each sip was a spark, like confetti delight,
We munched on sweet laughter, absurdly out of sight.

Marshmallows danced on the edge of our cups,
As we flew through the night, no time for hiccups.
With a whirl and a twirl, oh the stories we spun,
Like vines of sweet memories, tangled and fun.

Under blankets of stars, we savored our dreams,
While the pillows erupted with giggly moonbeams.
The warmth of our hearts kept the chill far away,
As we toasted to fun on this marvelous day.

So here's to the moments that tickle our glee,
With flavorful sips as light as the sea.
In cozy conditions, where smiles overflow,
May laughter keep brewing, and friendships still grow.

## **Sweet Fireside Serenade**

In a chair that creaks and squeaks,
I sip my brew while laughing seeks.
The flames they dance, they twist, they twirl,
I swear they wink at me, oh girl!

The teddy bear beside me grins,
As we debate which toast wins.
Should it be marshmallows divine,
Or maybe cookies dipped in wine?

Cats prance around, oh what a sight,
Chasing shadows, giving a fright.
A squirrel might sneak in for a snack,
But I've got my treats, no turning back!

So gather round, let laughter flow,
With every crackle, let joy grow.
For by this glow, we find our cheer,
In a world where winter is just a veneer.

## Whimsies of the Winter Night

The chill outside is quite a tease,
But here inside, I do as I please.
A cup of warmth in hand I cling,
While goofy thoughts make my heart spring.

With mismatched socks and a fuzzy hat,
I jiggle and wiggle, imagine a cat.
It chases snowflakes with all its might,
While I toast my feet by the glowing light.

The bookshelf quakes at my laughter loud,
As I hum to the tunes of the holiday crowd.
But the best part, oh, I must confess,
Is how my dog thinks he's the best chef!

He sneaks some snacks from the table near,
His guilty face as he seems to steer.
Yet with each nibble, my heart feels right,
In this funny dance of the winter night.

## The Heartbeat of an Ember's Light

With every crack, I hear a tale,
Of chocolate dreams that never fail.
The wood snaps back, in playful jest,
As shadows prance and take their rest.

A circle blooms where laughter thrives,
Sipping treasures brings us alive.
The glow reveals my friend's old hat,
Which turns heads, not just from the cat!

Spontaneous songs begin to soar,
As some wise guy joins in once more.
We mock the cold and battle the frost,
While our silly fun counts for the lost.

So here we sit, all cozy and bright,
In the rhythm of the ember's light.
Where winter's chill can't steal our glee,
We'll dance along, just wait and see!

## **Mugs Raised Under Starry Skies**

Our mugs are filled, the stars align,
With every sip, it's all divine.
We laugh and toast to frosty twirls,
As the night unfolds, it gently swirls.

The moon peeks down with a sly grin,
While stirring dreams of mischief within.
Should we build a snowman or start a fight?
A snowball blast under soft moonlight!

The canines bark, they leap and bound,
While we sip and giggle without a sound.
Every splash and fumble is pure delight,
In this zany gathering of winter's night.

So let's not fret about the chill,
With mugs held high, our hearts will fill.
For under this vast, star-filled dome,
We find our fun, we feel at home!

Milton Keynes UK
Ingram Content Group UK Ltd.
UKHW022011131124
451149UK00013B/1100

9 789916 944073